MY PENNING VOYAGE

R GAYATHRI

I wholly dedicated this book to my parents ,family members ,friends and all the supporters who encouraged me to do my best in expressing my thoughts in a correct way .

Contents

Contents

Contents

Contents

Contents

Disclaimer

This wonderful collection of 100 poems contain writeups on various topics. The writeups are the author's original content. The author guarantees that the content is piracy free.

Foreword

Mr.A.Ramalingam ,M.A,M.Ed, M.Phil (English)HM (RETD)KRISHNAGIRI DT

I feel exhilarated to go through the poems of the young poetess, Mrs Gayathri Devi. The poems are artistically self sufficient and alike in form .Its content is powerful and conveys the total effect.

Though they may not be the mighty lines of Marlow, this will earn you unique place among the learned people.

The Style and versification suffer in quality in comparison.

It shows the way of progress and the love for learning and passion of the Poetess.Beauty brings out the budding artists' emotion.

She has given firm footing to the ornate poetry , alongwith sureness, accuracy and variety.

Therefore ,there is a desire for elegance, correctness,simplicity and spontaneity.

The poetry is marked by some organic sensibility ending in powerful inspiration.

Her love for nature is found. The nature of the poems is to be enjoyed fully for its sensuous manner .

We can see in this legend of poems,all learned scholars' appreciation and one can enjoy the unfailing efforts of this young peacock Gayathri. Her poems add colourful wings to that peacock and I hope it will bring clouds and showers in the hearts of readers.

I hope she will be appreciated.

Let God shower her with blessings. Let her literary taste flourish.

Finally, a word to say that I am proud for having her as the best student in my teaching life.

Thank you .

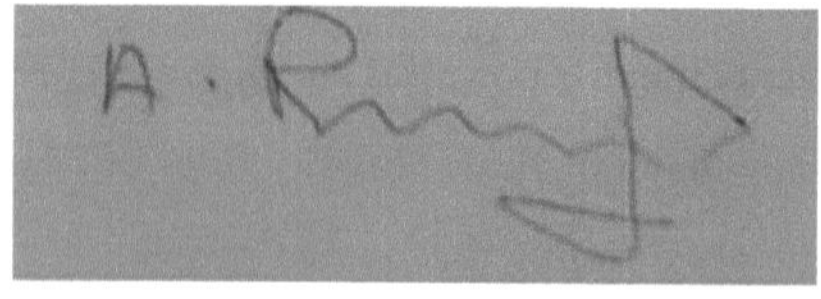

A.RAMALINGAM

FOREWORD

Foreword

Mrs. S. SUMATHI, M.A., B.Ed.,
SRI KGS HR. SEC. SCHOOL,
ADUTHURAI,
THANJAVUR DT.

Mrs. R. Gayathri, a friend of mine, as known to me is a very innovative and a lovable person. She is so caring as a mother and so energetic as a butterfly. She has always a thirst in learning new things. She is so dedicated to her profession and loved her students very much. She received block level and district

level "Best teacher award" as the recognition of her sincerity. Apart from this, she has been honoured with many awards. I came to know her only through the group of Creative Writers. Being a Maths teacher, her interest in literature makes me dumb founded. Creative writers is the best platform to express herself. Here too she showed her dedication by writing the poems without missing even a single day. As a result of that, here comes the book "My Penning Voyage."

She started the book with the writeup "Life is not a bed of roses", mentioning the twists and turns in life. She adviced to "Open our wings and fly" to reach our goals. She insisted the importance of learning in "The art of learning". As a patriotic lover of her nation she dreamt that her nation should be full of innovation. She spoke about how every human should be in her poem "Manners." She asked many questions to God in "Question to God." She requested everyone to "Keep Smiling",whatever happens in life. Her "Healing Mantra", was really awesome. She dedicated poems to her parents and siblings in "My super mom, my love", "My dad, my hero", and "Long live dear brothers and sisters." She explain "The power of discipline". She give a big "Salute to Doctors" through her writeup. She wrote about the ladders who uplift the society, "Teacher." She demonstrated that "True beauty" lies in selfless service. These are only some small illustrations from her writeups. Really I felt merry while reading the poems. All the poems are fantastic with nice rhyming words, rhyme scheme and some poetic devices. She has played very well with the verses. I

am sure her verses would make the readers love it.

Wish you more success.

S.SUMATHI

Preface

Poetry is , when an emotion is found its thought and the thought had found words .

- Robert Frost

The author of the book in the name of " My penning voyage " ,a collection of hundred poems had given the pleasure of reading a variety of topics. The way of expression is simple and vivid.

Acknowledgements

The mind is like a flower. It does not bloom without the lights of appreciation, encouragement and love.

- Debasish Mridha

From the depth of heart , I extend my gratitude to my family members for their support. I am very grateful to Mrs. D. Brinda Srinivas, Graduate Teacher (English) GHS,Melpattampakkam, Cuddalore Dt who has shown the platform of writing poems.

I extend my greatest pleasure to Mr.Ramalingam ,My Higher secondary school English teacher (Retd HM) native of Krishnagiri Dt and Mrs. S. Sumathi ,English teacher of Thanjavur Dt as well as author of two books "String of Pearls" and "Drizzling of Verses" for supporting me by giving the admiring foreword.

I sincerely convey my gratitude to Mrs.Jael Beulah , Mrs.P.R.Kalayani and Mr.S.Santhanam for providing their time in editing and drafting the book .

I'm always thankful for the CW family members for continuous reviews and appreciation and all who have supported me in publishing this book .

About The Athor

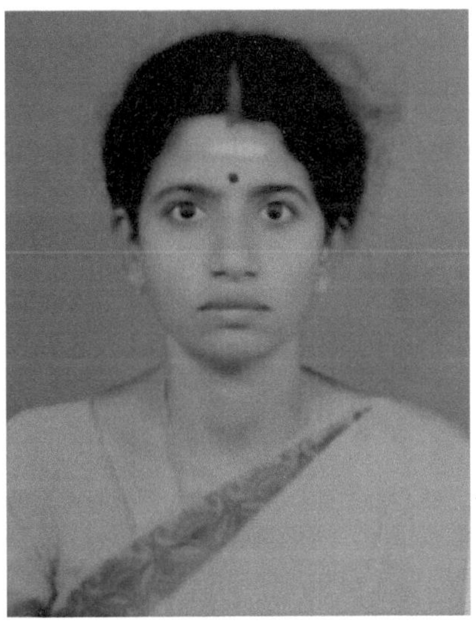

Mrs.R. Gayathri M.S.C,B.Ed.

Mrs.R. Gayathri was born on 1983 in Krishnagiri Dt. She has the degree of M.Sc (Maths) and B.Ed., She is working as a teacher since 2005 . She loves children very much. She is very kindhearted by her nature . Her hobbies are reading, writing and listening to music. This is the first attempt she tried to publish the book, a collection of simple hundred poems. She has completed around 400 poems after joining Creative Writers group on May5,2021.

She is a good teacher to her students. She is a good woman to the society. She is a receiver of Block level ,district level Best Teacher awards. She recieved an "Award of Excellence" by Kalam UV foundation. "Siranda Kalvi Sindanaiyalar" award for writing poems in cw group honoured by International Lion's club of Tiruvelneli.

She is the best human showing concern for all the creatures.

About The Book

Reading a book is like taking a journey.

- Emma Gulliford

Everything happens for a reason with God's grace. With the blessings of God, the author has taken an opportunity to bring out this book .

Hope the author makes everyone enjoy who touches her thoughts .

1. Life is Not a Bed of Roses

Smile and cry are the two sides of the life's coin.
Accept whatever comes to you without pain.
Success never calls you on its own.
Workhard; Don't postpone.
Twists in life may be awful.
Accept and be laurel.
Your life will be sweet like a choral.
Let your life teach moral.
Survive for the best.
Uncertainty happens as surprise test.
Always have a thirst for the quest.
Surely, you'll reach the crest.
Many wish for more needs.
Leading to mere deeds.
To have whatever is needful,
Is the truth of life for being successful.
Life is full of struggles and challenges.
Trust in God and believe yourself.
Life is not a bed of roses.
Life is a mixture of roses surrounded by thorns.

2. Open Your Wings And Fly

Open your wings and fly.
Like a bird to reach high.
There is no limits to touch the sky.
Let our hearts always try.
Open your wings and fly.
Like a kite in the open sky.
Let your goals be higher.
To make your life easier.
Open your wings and fly like a flight.
It's a beautiful sight.
Everyone looks at you with excellent credit.
Flying exactly by the goal,makes you perfect.

3. One Day I Will..

Though my path has many obstacles.
I learned to walk with my smiles.
Though my life is filled with ups and downs.
I realized, my happiness lies in others.
Instead of searching for my joyfulness ,
I transformed my heart to bring others by happiness.
The world seek for true hearts and helping hands.
I want to be the one to share my hands.
Spreading out the fullest happiness among many children.
One day I will be like Mother Teresa to love and help the needy children.

4. The Art Of Learning

The passion for living
Is the art of learning .
Every living being learns by practice.
It gives you the pleasure and an experience.
Learning differs from each other.
But the desire of learning is same.
It gives an individual self satisfaction
And also recognition.
From cradle to graveyard, learning is continuous.
It prevents us from being monotonous.
Learning skills give you confidence.
It helps us live with determination.

5. Learn To Say No

Practice our children to have confidence.
Realize the truth with acceptance.
Always, there is no need for unwanted patience.
Sometimes, anything disturbs your surveillance.
Oppose the situation with impatience.
Say no for the disguising faces.
Tear up the mask, chase away from you.
Safeguard yourself.
Everyone not speak with good morality.
Teach them a lesson in reality.
Saying no is the precautionary measure.
To protect our children from incidental abuse.

6. Why Me?

Life is all about moving forward.
Don't blame yourself for silly reasons too.
Always a controversy over mind and heart,
When an incident broadens the thought.
Love yourself with courage.
Everyday is to enjoy and encourage.
When a question comes "why me?",
Answer immediately," why not me?"
Nothing is permanent in the world.
For every problem, there is a solution to find.
There is a reason for sudden change.
Learn properly how to manage.
When everyone hopes for the first,
Who will be looking for the rest?
Whatever comes to you next,
Forget "Why me?" and your life will be the best.

7. My Dreams For My Nation

My dreams for my nation,
Is not just a fashion.
It's like a passion for my nation.
To bring everyone by compassion.
My dreams for my nation,
Is full of innovation.
Everyone has a decision.
Let it bring a renovation.

8. Rainbow Of Feelings

I asked God to define life?
He silently said,"look at the sky right".
Oh!There appeared a rainbow ray of light.
To enlighten me, something bright.
Heartfully I realized life is made of feelings.
Rainbow speaks of many things.
Happiness and sadness appear and disappear.
It often comes in the human life sphere.
Success and failures are not permanent.
Enjoy everyday in your life as a tenant.
Aims and goals should be broader.
Think high to cross the border.
Life lies in colorful surprises.
Fly out like pretty butterflies.
Human life span may be short.
Be friendly with every heart.

9. Do Small Things With Great Love

Little bit of time saves many lives ,
When the doctor takes risk for the patients.
Little drops of rain from the sky,
Keeps the land wet from becoming dry.
Little amount of money saved,
Is very helpful in difficulty.
Little food for the hungry people,
Satisfies the hungry from being starved.
Doing little things with true heart,
Makes yourself happy and satisfied.
Little things done with great love,
Drives out vengeance from our hearts.
Spread the seeds of love.
Water that with kindness.
Often clean the weeds of selfishness.
Let the world be filled with blossoming flowers of selflessness.

10. Life Is Full Of Contradictions

Human beings seek for happiness.
But sometimes ends up in sadness.
Expectation is the reason for life's alterations.
Experience the happenings as life's best medications.
Even the road needs speed brakers,
In-between to minimize the risks.
How can be the life without contradictions?
It's a monotonous journey of life without thrillings.
Life is full of contradictions.
Accept and adjust is my suggestion.
Avoiding and annoying will not give any solution.
Experience the life as a recollection.

11. Manners

Manners make a man.
With good morals, do all you can.
Being trustworthy all the time,
Patience in every situation is mine.
Respect others with courage.
Showing gratitude in all the stage.
Integrity with all.
Love others without fall.
Respect others' opinion.
Never try to impose your opinion.

12. Ramzan!A festival of charity

Every good deed is a charity.
Every charitable action takes you towards heaven.
Give and you will receive,
Is a sense of happiness.
Charity purifies mind and soul,
Feels humble and thankful.
It brings Patience and perseverance.
Understands human suffering.
Charity may be tiny,
Worth than a penny.
When Allah blesses you financially,
Don't raise your own standard of living.
Raise your standard of giving.

13. The way I took was different

God has given me a wonderful birth.
I started realizing my heart's worth.
Beauty is felt through eyes.
Hospitality takes us many miles.
Realize all with genuine love and care.
Every heart expects to survive.
Smile at everyone unconditionally.
Be kind to the world.
Hands shaken with wishes are everywhere.
But helping hands to cherish is very rare.
The way I took was different.
To see the world with my heart.

14. Question to God

Disparity in the society.
Humans feel insatiety.
Populace cry for pacification.
People search for gratification.
In our prosperity and adversity,
Let nature brings symmetry.
Everything happens by chance,
Resulting in chaotic occurrence.
As you (God) witnessed,
Ours arrival to the Earth.
Why are we here?
What is our mistake?
When will you pacify us?

15. This too shall pass away

The world we look around today,
Seems dull due to pandemic.
Humans struggle to breathe,
Though oxygen is plenty in nature.
Scientists are increasingly more,
But the exact medication is not found there.
Picnics have become rare.
Staying at home scared.
The festive and family celebrations stopped at home.
So sharing and caring others via phone.
Nothing is permanent in the world.
Of course, this too shall pass away...

16. Keep smiling

Life is all about,
The ups and downs happening a while.
The good and bad times occur like a dice.
The peaks and valleys are not alike.
Tears and laughter, we compromise.
Life is all about moving with a smile.
Accept everything as a trial.
Smiling keeps you live longer.
So keep smiling forever.

17. Dear moon,you remind me of...

Oh!Glittering moon,
You remind me ..
The dark sky at night.
My presence makes it bright.
When you are right.
Your life will be polite.
Wear and tear, my life's nature.
So, face the truth without pressure.
Your life is a sculpture.
Day by day, shape yourself for the future.
Everybody look at me up.
As my shining always gleams up.
You lift our heart as spring lifts up.
Your life will be a sweet syrup.

18. Music man..Mr.Ilayaraja

Your voice is unique.
You touch us by rhythmic technique.
Your special vibration of voice.
Brings everlasting rejoice.
Even your silent humming,
Singing inside is heart touching.
You are a remarkable person.
Breathe in the hearts with a rhythmic passion.

19. My healing mantra is...

My healing mantra is Patience..

Pray for everyone.

All we need is cooperation.

This too shall pass away.

It's true in the life journey.

Everything happens for a reason.

No need to worry.

Care about the current situation.

Everyday gives you an opportunity.

Move each day by a new way.

Hope you are blessed in the world to stay.

Accept the situations with tolerance.

20. I got stunned by..

Everyday the sun's restless shine,
Seems everyone to wake earlier.
Making us feel alive ,
Every second the trees produce oxygen.
The birds and animals care their young ones,
Though they have five senses.
Everything in the world,
Is nature's charitable gift.
I got stunned by nature,
Which has the endless treasures.
Enjoying with pleasure,
I am living amidst of the nature.

21. Forgiveness, Thy name is women

Forgiveness is a wonderful gift to receive.
Everybody doesn't have a generous heart to give.
Often mistakes happen at home unexpectedly.
Mothers handle them gently.
Forgiveness relieves the pain caused by anger.
When there is a hand or a shoulder to hold on.
Sorry is a short and sweet word.
Suddenly makes one's heart feel secured.
Forgiveness shows the mercy,
Not to hold the offence.
One Mother Teresa is enough to perceive,
"Forgiveness, thy name is women. "

22. My inner voice

I have a voice, for tuning my heart.
When I go right, it tells correct.
When I go wrong, it warns me to be calm.
Though I am quiet, that whispers day along.
Either it comes from my heart or brain.
It runs out like a train.
My inner voice, always acts like a hero.
When I am not listening, that makes me zero.

23. My super mom,My love

Your heart is filled with care.
Always you will share.
Your love is precious.
So, I stand speechless.
You helped me to grow.
And taught whatever you know.
You never said no for me.
That spirit lead me with courage.
A dictionary is not enough to define you.
You mean so much to me.
I love you forever,
My gorgeous heart, mother.

24. My dad,My hero

Dad is not a word to define.
You are a man of divine.
You are so innocent.
You made my life pleasant.
You are always silent.
You made my life a better event.
You are the sky of my life,
With your blessings my life thrive.

25. Long live dear brothers and sisters

My dear brothers and sisters,
Beloved Vivekanananda's voice.
Calling anyone as brother or sister,
Brings a bond of care and happiness.
Either younger or elder in age,
They accompany the best in all the stage.
Sharing the life as a better half.
Caring with a cheerful laugh.
My dear brothers and sisters,
Live long life with good health and pleasure.
You show me the right way,
My heart always pray.

26. The power of discipline

Discipline is the key to life.
Reshapes our life.
Practicing good habits to transform our life.
Builds better relationships with tolerance.
Parents teach us good habits.
Till we realize the moral traits.
Gives confidence in all aspects.
To achieve right things with quest.
Teachers train us to gain good morality.
Sometimes, we feel it hard to do our duty.
But lifelong their strictness improves our self esteem.
We can even manage the matters under the team.
Friends oppose when we commit mistakes.
It may be not tolerable a little while.
It reshapes our behavior endlessly.
Start making decisions very keenly.
The power of discipline is
Like a light that glows brightly.
When you practise regularly,
Life sparkles effortlessly.

27. I feel sad but I don't know why?

Whenever I cross the street,
Anyone expects food to eat
Or animals search food in hunger.
I feel their pain tougher.
Whenever I travel in the bus ,
Anyone searches for empty seat in stress.
I worry for them forgetting my smile ,
When they stand for a long while.
Whenever I look at oldage homes and orphanages,
I am concerned about their happiness.
I should show my kindness.
They are living to seek tenderness.
Though I am blessed
With enough pleasures in the world,
I feel sad for others untold sufferings
And I don't know why...

28. A flying kite

A kite flying in the sky,
Cut off from the thread tied.
Met my hands with shaking.
Conveying a message of hoping.
The children are fond of making a kite.
They play for a long time.
A kite flies very high.
It tells be conscious about the life.
A kite reminds of aim.
Even be conscious about time.
Luck favors sometime.
But hardwork assists all the time.

29. There is a limit for my patience

Dear human beings,
I have given you enough freedom,
To enjoy the life without boredom.
But you made me bitter,
By making the nature's land worst.
I have given you a plenty of water everywhere.
To survive without thirst for future.
But you made me contaminated,
By throwing chemicals fainted.
Trees around the surrounding areas,
Provide oxygen to breathe.
But you cut them endlessly ,
So breathing air is decreasing tremendously.
There is a limit for my patience,
It is a caution for your innocence..
Keep an end for your selfishness.
Otherwise a new disease will make you more dangerous

30. I can't live without..

I can't live without my children.
Because they make my heart strengthen.
Their silly talks often,
Makes me feel soften.
Their surprise action of little things,
Makes me fly with pretty wings.
They are the meaning of my life.
Without their presence,
I can't believe me alive.

31. Strange habits

Due to the pandemic lockdown situation.
People stick to mobile phones often.
Either message is there or not.
The curiosity arises in brain's spot.
Nowadays maximum of the children,
Not liked to play outdoor games.
Addicted to play online games.
Spend a lot of time with mobile.
Forgetting the life's routine.
Systematic life has been altered.
There is no freedom, unexplained.
When we forget to train up today,
There will be complaints everyday.
The root cause of today's children strange habits
Should be modified by regular practice.
Otherwise the forthcoming generation,
Will be spoiled physically and mentally.
Restyle the children's life,
For prominent progress.

32. Sport man spirit

Practice makes a man perfect.
A familiar quote for sport man spirit.
Each day struggles hard.
To reach out the goal of the sky.
Shaping up their life as a sport man,
Is not an easy task as win.
Sacrificing most of the happiness,
Leads to the perfection.
Either the winner or the runner,
Receiving a medal will be the best for the beginner.
Hope for the star.
You can win the star.

33. Salute to Doctors

When we feel sick,
Need a remedial trick.
Home remedies never help all the time.
A best medicine is needed at that time.
We pray for good health and wealth.
Sometimes we lack our hope of health.
We visit the doctor for healing.
To check out the reason for suffering.
A doctor works selflessly,
To save the lives of the humanity.
They treat the patients hourly.
We have to thank them daily.
The doctors never mind their lives.
Though they have the family to survive.
Many doctors sacrificed their breathe,
Due to pandemic crisis.
The doctors are the living God.
Care and make us free from feeling hard.
Salute to all the doctors,
The precious life's saviors.

34. Gallery of my heart

My heart is like a tree.
I want to be depression free.
I pour out hope and faithful thoughts.
To grow well with positive attitudes.
I get the fruits of good relationships with comfort.
I removed the weeds of negativity.
I pray for peace and tranquility .
Let me spread good deeds to nurture.

35. Grief disappears when..

When my heart felt sad,
I felt little hard.
Just I went out for a walk.
There I observed few children talk.
What a gleeful moment!
My heart changed at the spot.
A garden of beautiful flowers,
Smiling always without worries.
A group of stars,
Twinkling without bars.
A flock of birds,
Flying beyond the sky limits.
My grief disappears,
Whenever I cross the beaming kids.

36. I miss these things the most in my life..

Human's nature is when anything comes near,
Taking it easy without fear.
When it runs out of hands,
Worrying about it and demand.
I am not exceptional to that.
My little carelessness changed my career thought.
Though my heart satisfies,
Mind insists you have missed the better opportunities.
Expectation has no limits.
Sometimes mind reminds missed things.
As the life's way moves..
Everything vanishes.
Human's nature is when anything comes near,
Taking it easy without fear.
When it runs out of hands,
Worrying about it and demand.
I am not exceptional to that.
My little carelessness changed my career thought.
Though my heart satisfies,
Mind insists you have missed the better opportunities.
Expectation has no limits.
Sometimes mind reminds missed things.

As the life's way moves..

Everything vanishes.

37. Consolation

Whenour heart feels heavy,
We need a support for our life.
Few words from the dear ones,
Vanish the pain caused by the difficulty.
Everyone stands for the care and comfort ,
As the failures cannot be resolved.
Searching for a better half of the life,
To share the bitter experience.
There needs a heart for consolation.
That may be the one who is genuine.
Gives shoulder to forget the sadness.
You be the generous heart to console the world.

38. Teacher

Teachers are the real heroes.
Dedicates their life for the children's lives.
Every little action speaks much.
They accompany the best in touch.
Ladders for uplifting the society.
Sacrificing for the better community.
Teaching out to reach high.
To make the Nation as the best.
Encouragement for the students.
Brings the society with worth personalities.
Makes many lives colourful.
Teachers, we are very thankful.
Teachers are the real heroes.
Dedicates their life for the children's lives.
Every little action speaks much.
They accompany the best in touch.
Ladders for uplifting the society.
Sacrificing for the better community.
Teaching out to reach high.
To make the Nation as the best.
Encouragement for the students.
Brings the society with worth personalities.
Makes many lives colourful.

Teachers, we are very thankful.

39. Get well soon

Dear God,
We human beings trust you forever.
When we struggle to live further.
Every obstacle happens for better living.
We hope you to cross the hurdles with your blessing.
Save everyone with good health.
We pray for physical and mental strength.
Thank you God.
We have hope in you.

40. When I look back now, I realized..

Life is not worrying about the past.
It's better to satisfy with the rest.
Always every heart expects the best.
God has already given a test.
Every experience is a contest.
Accept the result as right.
Heart will be quiet.
Fly out like a kite.
When I look back now, I realized
To live without unwanted pressure as my life is a treasure.

41. Pillars to create pillars of the society..

Little stones together make a big rock.
Little drops of the water make the ocean.
Little action of good deeds make a big impact.
Little plants after growing endow many fruits.
Little kids shaped with right model,
Make the Nation worthy of living.
Little minds cultivated with responsible thoughts,
Make the Nation respected everywhere.
The teachers of selfless service,
Is the pillars to create the pillars of the society.
They should be respected by everyone,
In the hearts of the society.

42. You can only manage yourself

You can only change yourself.
You are unique by self.
Don't think of the hurdles.
Think about the life's riddle.
Each has an exact solution.
That lies in your perception.
Your destiny is written by you.
So you can only change yourself.
Life is a mixture of unexpected situations.
Each defines the different experiences.
One's path is defined by oneself.
You are the one and only one to can change yourself.

43. Eat nicely

Food brings the joy of satisfaction,
When you serve anyone with love and affection.
The food gets more taste than its ingredients.
A smile and a word a little more to the guests.
Add a crown to the hearts.
Food is the only thing whenever served,
After sometime enough is the word uttered.
It brings more happiness.
To both the server and the receiver.
Requesting eat nicely is the noblest culture of Indians.

44. The God replied

There is a conversation between my mind and heart.
Argument was going on without an end of art.
Why people are struggling for so much of things.
Even though they have enough ways to satisfy with the possibilities.
Suddenly a peace of mind and heart.
Heard a mild voice from the God.
God replied, "It's karma of the action."
Be good and do good is the truthful action.
Many human beings forget that.
Though they have the six senses of realization.
What you will do, will come to you in time
The real truth of life.
Atlast, God finalized,
Be aware of good deeds for others.
Remember Newton's third law,
"For every action ,
There is an equal and opposite reaction."

45. The show must go on..

Everyday starts with its own scene.
The show must go on till the journey declines.
Some are made of smiles.
Some are made of cries.
Some days are thrilling.
Some days are tragic.
Time doesn't wait for anyone.
The show must go on.
Don't worry about anything.
Act yourself better in the show.
Till your breathe continues,
The show must go on.
Do the best you can.
Love everyone as you can.
Share your life with others.
It must go on without disturbances.

46. Wings..

Birds are peculiar creatures.
Fly very high and fast.
Adapt to the environment.
Attracts the human by attachment.
Wings help them to fly higher.
Safeguard themselves from horror.
Each bird is special in the nature.
They should live without human pressure.

47. Books ..

Books are good friends.
Read by the readers.
Knowledge thirst is different.
Book feeds for betterment.
Learning starts from cradle.
Books are the support like a ladder.
As much you read, that makes you gain.
Books are like lifelong train.
Choose the right one for your life.
Everything is possible for you.
Books make you knowledgeable.
That makes you perfect and complete.

48. Life is to live...

Problems are common to all.
Realize yourself and all.
When you see others pain as yours,
There is no reason for ego, anger and mistakes.
Ants don't have desire to live "butterflies" life.
Elephants never imagine to fly in the sky.
Why some people are jealous of others?
Everyone is unique by God's creativity.
You are rich and beautiful by grace.
Don't loose your time by thinking waste.
Don't be hatred of the life.
Life is to live! Life is to live!

49. Is it possible for me?

Every individual is born to be unique.
Learn to follow the right way of principle.
Never give up hope,
Even when you get failures.
"Participation is important" than failures.
When you are born as a human being,
Achieve the goals should be your motto.
Many great personalities work hard,
To enjoy the fruits of the success.
When you think possible,
Everything is possible for you.
Don't underestimate your strength.
It's possible for you in the Earth.

50. Be happy

Love the darkness, you can see the light.
Love the failure, you can realize the success.
Love the work, you can grow.
Love yourself and you can understand the world.
Nothing is in our hands.
Trust yourself in the world.
Life consists of miseries.
Don't mind that seriously.
When you lose everything,
Tomorrow is there for you to withstand.
No one is without queries.
Try to reduce the queries.

51. Looking at the past

Looking at the past of the life,
Reminds evergreen moments.
Number of people, So many changes
Crossed all the stages.
Many lovable persons lost their lives.
Dangerous diseases and disasters.
Realized the true hearts.
Money alone is not the best.
Satisfaction not lies outside.
Lies in your perception.
Looking at the past of the life,
Reminds life is a puzzle.

52. Foot prints

The stages of life reminds many foot prints.
When I was a child of little age,
Many foot prints I have seen around me.
Father and mother hold me together,
Wherever I go for my happiness.
As I moved as a girl,
My friends were there to share and care.
When I became a grown up,
Followed by many foot prints.
I practiced my heart and mind to walk alone.
Foot prints are unique,
Like my thoughts about the life.
Let me follow up the right path.

53. Physical education period..

A flock of birds flying in the sky.
There is no limits to fly.
They never feel shy.
They are not ready to say good bye.
Echoing with the friends.
No restriction for the students.
Enjoying with the empty foots.
Playing of their choices.
Everyone wants to enjoy that.
No one denies the outside world set.
Many trophies are waiting for the students.
A lively place to identify the real players.

54. The plea of a teacher, No work no pay..

Teacher's profeession is the noblest.
By satisfying student's knowledge thirst.
Teachers are dedicated for the students.
Reshape each student as a beautiful statue.
A teacher is honored by student's nature.
As they are enriched with knowledge treasure .
The plea of a teacher is responsible for all.
They are the pillars of the society wall.
Respect teachers and teacher's service.
They stand like the ladders to serve us.
Teachers encourage from their heart.
By realizing the student's exact thought.
No work no pay, is not a right way to say.
It's time to thank them by the way.
A matchstick can light up many candles.
A teacher can shine up many scholars.

55. Tommorrow

Everyone sleeps with the hope.
That they will wake up tomorrow.
Though a day of the life has ended.
Waiting for a tomorrow as blessed.
Always hope for a better tomorrow.
Don't postpone anything for tomorrow.
Hope brings confidence.
Postponing leads to laziness.
Tomorrow takes to more expectations.
Waiting for positive experiences.
It doesn't lie in your hands.
We are like dolls in the God's hands.

56. True beauty

True beauty lies in selfless service.
By little deeds of love.
That lies in inner heart,
Not in looking smart.
That lies in spreading out,
Little smile by our eyes .
True beauty lies in shining others life
By our good actions.

57. An empty nest

Birds lived in the trees as a home.
Is this identity still existing for them,
As an abode?
United they lived happy.
Shared their love beautifully.
Humans show the birds to their children.
For feeding and stop crying action.
Birds care their young ones as a protector.
But humans disturb them as a controller.
Birds spread seeds everywhere.
Humans enjoyed the fruitfulness of the trees.
They started to sell the nature,
By his selfish nature.
Our environment has lost the identity of many birds.
Many species of the birds vanished.
Plant a tree near your abode.
Let them rest at the home.
Keep some grains and water.
Let them have a life better.
Protect the trees,
As they won't remain as an empty nest.

58. It's better to be alone than..

When a heart gets impressed,
There faith and love are promised.
When a little misunderstanding occurred,
Turns out the heart to worry.
The situation becomes toughened.
The heart's distance gets lengthened.
To get the peace of mind..
It's better to be alone,
Than trusting all blindly.

59. Euphoric moment of my life

One day my work was tough.
I returned home very late.
There was no strength to cook.
But I felt very hungry intense look.
It was already eleven at night.
I asked my child,
Is there milk at home right now?
Just he brought a cup of milk.
Mom, have it.. he smiled.
With the biggest surprise,
That's the ecstasy.
I tasted with my child's intimacy.
Eyes filled with joy..
I was on cloud nine,
When he cared me like a child.
The best moment of my life.

60. Save nature to save you

Save the nature's soul.
To save the human soul.
Our ancestors lived,
A pollution free life.
We are living in a polluted atmosphere.
An impending danger for the future generation.
Polluting our mother nature,
Will spoil our future.
Disturbing our surroundings,
Will end up in death of life.
Save nature by planting trees.
To save the Earth from pollution.

61. You are my sunshine..

My friend,
When I am feeling glad,
you share my happiness.
When I am sad,
you heal my heart.
When I need spirit ,
you stand beside me as a gift.
When I need a support,
you are there as a valuable asset.
Your presence turns my day to happy rays.
You are the sunshine of my life.

62. A letter for you..

Valuable time never comes back.
Spend your time and effort in learning track.
Waking up and going to bed is not the best living.
Everyday you should shape up for worthy living.
Helping and loving others is humanity.
Live that way to recognize your identity.
Always be caring and kind.
Remember your wellwishers in the life.
Thank them for their precious supports in time.

63. Kamarajar, An eye opener

A man of simplicity,
Named for sincerity.
Education is the only thing to shape the world.
Shaped the poverty of many to get educated.
Never expected luxuries,
Spent everything for schools.
Kamarajar the eye opener of the poor society.
Profound knowledge with the highly educated society.

64. Don't forget to follow

Life is a suspense novel.
The climax is not yet done.
Anger is the poison of life.
Often mistakes you.
Be calm and peaceful.
Tomorrow is not defined.
Live today without any worries.
Follow patience and forgive..
Everyone for little mistakes.

65. Obstacles

Obstacles never stop you dear.
Never approach the situation with fear.
Everything happens for a reason.
Accept with patience without any confusion.
Hurdles bring you a better experience.
Bear the pain with a smile.
Everything vanishes as time changes.
Nothing can stop you, face with courage.

66. Liberty

I want to fly like a bird,
But my wings are tied.
My freedom is like a parrot,
Open out the cage to pick up the strip.
Looking the birds flying in the sky,
Sometimes feel when I will be free.
Oh! I realized, my wings are always free.
I only practiced to fly in the limits.
Let my wings be free.
Let my world be free.

67. To forget a friend

A trustworthy friend is very precious.
Lives forever as a treasury.
Not all gets that valuable gift.
Good behavior and understanding makes not to forget.
To forget a friend is not an easy thing.
She will live in my heart till it stops beating.
Living in her heart ,
Tender like bird's feathers.

68. Loneliness

Better be alone than having a bad company.
Sometimes that decides our life's destiny.
Do your work with sincerity.
That shows your individuality.
Loneliness makes you understand your real quality.
Realize your originality.
Live your life with unique identity.
Forgetting all the worries is the remedy.

69. Pleasure in self sacrifice

A candle lights as many lights as possible.
A pure heart sacrifice many pleasures for others.
Many leaders are the examples in the history.
For the pleasure lies in self sacrifice.
Though we are in discomfort,
Console someone elsewhere in pain.
Time will reduce the heart's strain.
Uttering little kind words of action.

70. Let's light the world

Let's light the world with prayers.
Every heart should be filled with hopes.
Let's light the world with positive thoughts.
Every individual should be living with essential needs.
Let's light the world with love and care.
There will be big impact in everyone's life.
Let's light the world with smile.
There will be peace everywhere.
Let's light the world with powerful Education.
To eradicate gender discrimination.
To remove superstitious beliefs.
To improve the rest in humanity.

71. Camera

Eyes capture beautiful scenarios.
Heart captures memorable thoughts.
Everything can't be kept in memories.
But many moments are treasures.
Look here and Smile please,
The same words uttered often.
That precious photos, When seen makes the heart soften.
Cameras make it possible ,
The valuable moments.
Reminding the bondable relationships.

72. I am scared of..

I am scared of rumors with imaginary ears.
Spreads very fast like air.
There is no limits for rumor.
Always tests people's humor.
Walls have ear is a proverb.
That's true, somebody enjoys with chirp.
Don't pass on rumors.
Respect others' humor.

73. I am unique..

Many lives mere life.
I like to be unique.
Steps of the life are not even.
Cross the way with smiling face.
Smile is Charlie Chaplin's way.
Sorrows hide in the hearts.
Give your smile to others.
Your life will move smoother.

74. Education

Education is a tool to measure the level of knowledge .
Education brings confidence to survive as the best.
It's like an ornament, adds beauty to the individual.
It makes many lives to bloom beautifully.
Education makes you knowledgeable.
It makes your life sweet and gentle.
It is a life long learning.
Makes you shine always.

75. Picnic

A picnic is often a happy technique.
Even a little change from residence is a better picnic.
Looking at the new people.
Learning something strange.
Each journey is different from the others.
But every place reminds evergreen moments.
Starting from the home.
Wonderful experiences.
Every time preferring different places.
Refreshing the individual life's tastes.
The happiest of life times.
The maximum memorable experiences.

76. Life becomes more meaningful..

Life becomes more meaningful,
When my heart is thoughtful.
A small deed for others,
Brings a joy of a bird flying with feathers.
Simply ending the day with regular works,
Won't be the meaningful tasks .
Living in someone's heart with good character.
Makes the life beautiful altogether.

77. When I saw your smile for the first time ..

When I saw your smile,
All my pains gone through miles.
An unexpected arrival in the world.
To make me happy untold.
You don't know what you were doing,
I realized the extent of enjoying.
Whenever you were smiling unknowingly,
I felt it's a beautiful sight everyday.
Like a rainbow, your smile appeared occassionly.
It made a bond unconditionally.
Your smile is always innocent dear boy,
Even when you are grown up as a guy.

78. Be like flowers..

Be like flowers ..
Bloom beautifully
Smile naturally
Cheer everyone
Never bear worries.
Live for others.
Be like flowers of selfless service..

79. Cross the barriers..

The path may be filled with thorns.
Don't hesitate to try the best.
A Spider tries as much as possible.
An ant hurry to carry particles.
As being a human, you are precious.
Walk with hope and faith till the journey.
The remarkable crown is yours.
Cross the barriers by strong confidence.

80. Missing pages of life..

Every page is remarkable.
Missing pages of life also memorable.
Every page is written in it's own way.
Not everyone will guess that exact way.
Hardwork wins most of the times.
Fate deserves sometimes.
Hardwork adds new pages of life.
Fate subtracts few pages of life.
Whether it's added or subtracted.
Live simply to the extent.
Your good deeds make a big impact.
Your difficulties will be torn up as the missing pages.

81. There is beauty in simplicity..

There is beauty in simplicity.
It's always better than atrocity.
Living for others is simplicity.
Living for ourselves brings individuality.
Many eminent persons lived simple.
They are still in the hearts as valuable.
Caring for others brings everlasting pleasure.
Being simple in the life is a sculpture.

82. Faith

When we trust someone and they make us fool,
At that time we realize the value of faith.
Some people may be in front of the eyes.
Some people behind the eyes.
Couldn't find faith in everyone...

83. Hope is a flower..

Hope is a flower.
Increases your will power.
Improves your brain power.
That's the greatest shower.
Hope is a flower with positive attitudes.
Make a garland of success.
Even the situation like see_saw game.
Always have the flower of hope to shine.

84. Initiative to all...

Lord Ganesha initiative to all.
Trusting wholeheartedly raising the life as tall.
A God of simplicity and successful.
Even a little prayer makes powerful .
Everything starts with your blessings.
Never got failures.
You are the God of success.
Even seen in the little things with bless.

85. My India,clean and green..

My India, clean and green.
It's time to make it clean.
Cleanliness makes environment free.
Plant more trees for pollution free.
India is a country named for agriculture.
Always keep it green with good texture.
Spread the seed balls everywhere.
Our Nation will be evergreen forever.
Minimize your artificial usage.
Maximize the natural resource.
Clean our Nation as a responsible citizen.
Always live proudly as an Indian citizen.

86. Life is like a bubble..

Life is like a bubble to blow.
Enjoy the beauty little slow.
Don't let it overflow.
Always have a thirst for life to know.
Make blows endlessly.
Some may make you joyful.
Some may make you sad.
Enjoy the little things of life tirelessly.

87. Nobody understands me better than..

Nobody understands me better than my heart.
Whenever I am depressed by thought.
My heart consoles myself with a friendly mood.
Hey! Don't worry, you can change this temporary mood.
Whenever I need a suggestion for my question.
My heart gives me a better solution.
Whenever I hope for the best.
My heart encourages me to the last minute.
Whenever I expect a response from anyone,
My heart instructs, don't expect anything from anyone.
You are the best among the rest.
Never estimate yourself as the least.

88. Modern teachers..

Chalk and talk is an old trend.
Systems and mobiles are today's trends.
Initiative to many people.
Motivator to many hearts.
Unique by generous nature.
Teaching out of the classroom.
Uploading the new innovations.
Appreciating everyone with better gifts.

89. Making a living bud to bloom..

Teachers are the real heroes of the world.
They can never be explained in a word.
Cultivating so many noble values.
Increase the moral value of every infant.
Never feeling jealous or envy of anyone.
Lifts up the lives of many people.
A child learns upto good qualities.
Survives and adapts with adjustment.
Sustains with acceptance.
That's possible only by the teacher,
Who makes the living (child)bud to bloom with good character.
Teachers are dedicated and rare.
They should be respected from the heart's core.

90. Silence

Silence doesn't lie in emptiness.
Lies in contentedness.
Not about worrying negatively.
Combining life's positivity.
Days may move on better.
Thinking remains greater.
Memories sound in the silence.
You can realize yourself in peace.
Many questions are answered by you.
Listen to your thoughts.
None other than you know the circumstances.
Silence grants reply for the unanswered questions.

91. The worst kind of suffering is...

Oh! God, Please look at the needy.
But many people are greedy.
Many don't have a little,
To eat completely three times a day.
The world needs generous hearts,
To feed the needed hands.
By one's carelessness,
A little may thrown into the garbage.
Saving money may safeguard your future.
Sharing food credits blessings unknowingly.
Wipe out the hunger by rich hearts.
Let the world be filled with hospitality.

92. Every cloud has a silver lining

The night time sky is dark.
Shines with bright stars.
Every failure teaches the steps of success.
Experience makes you more confident.
Even bitter neem flowers have little drops of honey.
Why can't your life be sweet?
Every missed opportunity teaches,
The right way of life.
Learn from everything.
There is a solution for every problem.
Face the problem with the possibilities.
Accept the result as the offer from God.

93. Life in lifeless

Mobile phone, nowadays became an essential part.
Though we are alone, carry it all over.
Sometimes we forget the fact,
That makes us remember the things.
A little object in the hands of everyone.
Lengthened the world of our lives.
Within the walls,
Broaden the thoughts.
We think a little, save more in that.
Without it's presence, many of us feel hopeless.
A good thing helps in needs.
Widens the knowledge.

94. The real wealth is...

The real wealth is
Showing mercy to all.
Showing gratitude towards all.
Caring attitude for all the creatures.
Concerning heart for others.
A support for God's children.
A hand for speechless creatures.
Save as much as blessings from all.
Give as much as blessings to everyone.
Human life itself is a great wealth.
Thank God and everyone by
Using your sixth sense.
Unlike other living beings, we are unique.

95. Lessons I learnt from the ants

Lessons I learnt from you..
Are lots of good not a few.
You are too small to look.
For hardwork a good example.
Save today for worry less tomorrow.
Try and try until you reach your target arrow.
Sincere in following the principles.
A man can learn much by observing your life.
Though you are small by physical nature.
Hold the things more than your strength.
Being uniform in the world,
Admire everyone by your great work.

96. Count your blessings

My parents are my first blessing.
Everything I got easily without struggling.
But I thought most of the times
Life is strange than anything .
Time can heal anything.
Now I am satisfied with everything.
I realized God had given me enough blessing.
Not only receiving is a blessing.
Even giving counts much.
Thank God and parents for numerous blessings.
I transform the same way to my dears.
So still I am alive,
It will continue without counting.

97. Have you been to someone's heart and memory?

Being human is a wonderful God's gift.
Listening to the heart more than the mind.
Giving ears to the worrying hearts.
Spending time with the animals and birds.
Speaking with everyone without partiality.
Without expecting, showing the best in humanity.
Living in the world is usual here.
Living in the hearts always make us unique.
A smiling face, when receiving the food.
A cut puppy wagging the tails, when the food is served.
A bird eating the grains,
There a heart gets recognition.

98. A day of life

Start a day with prayer.
Make sure you are right.
Never compare.
In your perception, shine bright.
Smile a little.
Talk humble.
Don't be a riddle.
Don't raise you in trouble.
End the day with prayer.
Make yourself pure by thought.
Tomorrow is there to prepare.
Live with kind heart.

99. Pass on the light of Diwali

Pass on the light of Diwali.
To brighten the world with prosperity.
Let the darkness of human lives be removed ,
By the light of good hearts.
Let's encourage the society,
By holding the hands together.
Let's have a motto,
To improve the lives of the poor.
Let's hope that oldage homes be closed.
Let the future generations know,
The treasure of grand parents.
There should be no orphanages.
Let's light the lives of everyone,
To realize the humanity is there.
Support everyone and everywhere.
Let's pass on the light of mutual love.

100. Math genius Ramanujam

Making Mathematics meaningful.
Showed your interest in Mathematics, beautiful.
Lived a very short time.
Achieved more in the life time.
Born as a Tamilian.
Recognized all over the world.
There is no life without calculations.
You have solved many difficult equations.
A mind with knowledge treasure.
A man remembered by all the time.
A great maths genius of our Nation.
We should be proud of you.
Your birthday is recognized as a remarkable day.
From 2012, National Mathematics day.
Nature and human life is a mixture of Mathematics.
The great Ramanujam, known for Mathematical tricks.

Printed by Libri Plureos GmbH in Hamburg, Germany